Everything you need to know about
DINOSAURS
AND OTHER PREHISTORIC CREATURES

DK

Written by John Woodward
Consultant Darren Naish

DK London
Senior editor Shaila Brown
Senior art editor Vicky Short
US Editor John Searcy
Jacket editor Manisha Majithia
Jacket designer Laura Brim
Jacket design development manager
Sophia M.T.T.
Producer, preproduction Adam Stoneham
Producer Alice Sykes
Managing editor Paula Regan
Managing art editor Owen Peyton Jones
Publisher Sarah Larter
Art director Phil Ormerod
Associate publishing director Liz Wheeler
Publishing director Jonathan Metcalf

DK Delhi
Senior editor Vineetha Mokkil
Senior art editor Devika Dwarkadas
Editors Neha Pande, Priyaneet Singh
Art editors Sanjay Chauhan,
Rakesh Khundongbam
Assistant art editor Vanya Mittal
DTP designers Neeraj Bhatia, Dheeraj Singh
Managing editor Rohan Sinha
Deputy managing art editor Sudakshina Basu
Preproduction manager Pankaj Sharma
DTP manager Balwant Singh
Picture researcher Sumedha Chopra

First American Edition, 2014
Published in the United States by DK Publishing
1450 Broadway, Suite 801, New York, NY 10018

Copyright © 2014 Dorling Kindersley Limited
DK, a Division of Penguin Random House LLC
20 21 22 10 9 8 7 6
015—192748—Feb/14

A catalog record for this book is available from
the Library of Congress.

ISBN 978-1-4654-1575-2

DK books are available at special discounts when
purchased in bulk for sales promotions, premiums,
fund-raising, or educational use. For details, contact:
DK Publishing Special Markets, 1450 Broadway, Suite 801,
New York, NY 10018
SpecialSales@dk.com.

Printed and bound in China.

For the curious

www.dk.com

Smithsonian Institution

This trademark is owned by the Smithsonian
Institution and is registered in the U.S. Patent
and Trademark Office.

Consultant: Mike Brett-Surman, PhD, Museum
Specialist for Fossil Dinosaurs, Reptiles,
Amphibians, and Fish at the National Museum
of Natural History, Smithsonian Institution

Established in 1846, the Smithsonian
Institution—the world's largest museum and
research complex—includes 19 museums and
galleries and the National Zoological Park. The
total number of objects, works of art, and
specimens in the Smithsonian's collection is
estimated at 137 million. The Smithsonian is a
renowned research center, dedicated to public
education, national service, and scholarship in
the arts, sciences, and history.

CONTENTS

The **dinosaurs** that lived in the distant past were the most spectacular creatures to ever walk the Earth.

Some were **HUGE**, bigger than any other land animal that has ever lived.

Pachycephalosaurus

Many had dramatic **horns, spikes, and frills** for defense and show.

Sauropelta

Carcharodontosaurus

Others had **terrifying teeth** and **claws** for killing their prey.

Archaeopteryx

Alxasaurus

Some even had *feathers* to keep their bodies warm.

Sinornithosaurus

Apatosaurus

Ichthyornis

Suchomimus

And most amazingly, it is now clear that **not all dinosaurs *are* extinct.**

The survivors live all around us, as BIRDS.

5

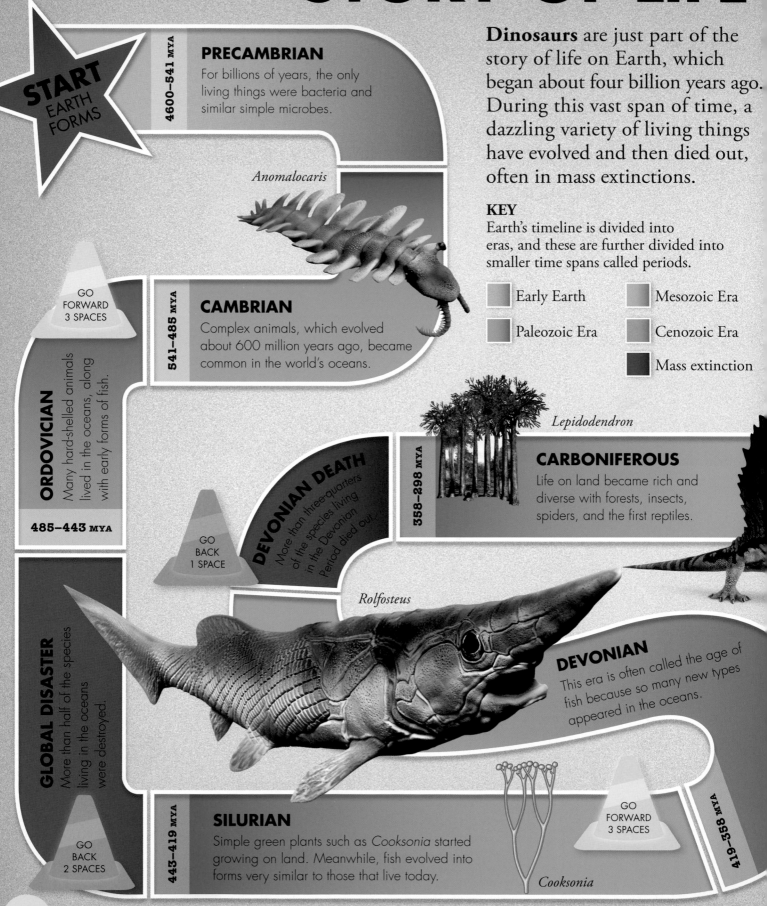

Dinosaurs are just part of the story of life on Earth, which began about four billion years ago. During this vast span of time, a dazzling variety of living things have evolved and then died out, often in mass extinctions.

KEY
Earth's timeline is divided into eras, and these are further divided into smaller time spans called periods.

- Early Earth
- Paleozoic Era
- Mesozoic Era
- Cenozoic Era
- Mass extinction

START
EARTH FORMS

PRECAMBRIAN
4600–541 MYA

For billions of years, the only living things were bacteria and similar simple microbes.

Anomalocaris

CAMBRIAN
541–485 MYA

Complex animals, which evolved about 600 million years ago, became common in the world's oceans.

GO FORWARD 3 SPACES

ORDOVICIAN
485–443 MYA

Many hard-shelled animals lived in the oceans, along with early forms of fish.

Lepidodendron

CARBONIFEROUS
358–298 MYA

Life on land became rich and diverse with forests, insects, spiders, and the first reptiles.

DEVONIAN DEATH
More than three-quarters of the species living in the Devonian Period died out.

GO BACK 1 SPACE

Rolfosteus

DEVONIAN
419–358 MYA

This era is often called the age of fish because so many new types fish appeared in the oceans.

GLOBAL DISASTER
More than half of the species living in the oceans were destroyed.

GO BACK 2 SPACES

SILURIAN
443–419 MYA

Simple green plants such as *Cooksonia* started growing on land. Meanwhile, fish evolved into forms very similar to those that live today.

GO FORWARD 3 SPACES

Cooksonia

NEOGENE

Modern types of birds and mammals appeared. The ancestors of humans evolved on the plains of Africa.

Argentavis

23–2 MYA

QUATERNARY

Humans spread around the globe as a series of ice ages gave way to the modern world.

Uintatherium

You will need:

- Dice
- One or more friends to play with
- A small object to use as a counter for each person

PALEOGENE

Birds survived and flourished, while mammals evolved rapidly to take the place of the large dinosaurs.

GO FORWARD 2 SPACES

66–23 MYA

BITTER END

The giant dinosaurs vanished.

GO BACK 2 SPACES

CRETACEOUS

The first flowering plants appeared, along with some of the most spectacular dinosaurs.

Archaeanthus

145–66 MYA

PERMIAN

Mammal ancestors appeared, while reptiles flourished in the dry desert climate.

298–252 MYA

Dimetrodon

How to Play:

The player who rolls the highest number goes first. When it's your turn, roll the dice and move the counter along by the number rolled, following the directions on the traffic cones. The first player to land on the last square wins!

JURASSIC

Dinosaurs evolved into many giant forms. They became the dominant animals on land.

THE BIG HIT

A global catastrophe eliminated almost all life on Earth.

GO BACK TO START

252–201 MYA

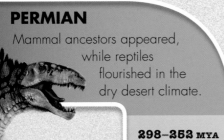

Peteinosaurus

GO BACK 3 SPACES

TRIASSIC

As life slowly recovered, the first dinosaurs, pterosaurs, and true mammals evolved.

RIVALS DIE OUT

Most dinosaur competitors were wiped out.

201–145 MYA

Guanlong

FINDING FOSSILS

Everything we know about **dinosaurs** comes from studying their **fossils**. Some are the **remains** of body parts like *bones and teeth*, buried so long ago that they have turned to STONE. Many fossils are **found by accident**. Even scientists who know *where to look* often find fossils that **surprise** them.

Fossilized shark tooth

Fossil fern frond

There are many different types of fossils that provide scientists with important clues about the past. Try this maze to find some fascinating fossils yourself.

START HERE

Fossil mold

A fossil mold forms when an animal is pressed into mud that turns to stone. This one shows a **trilobite**, a long-extinct sea creature.

Petrified wood

Trees that have been turned to stone preserve tree rings that show how they grew. Dinosaurs may have eaten the leaves of these trees.

Dinosaur tracks

The three toes of this footprint show it was made by a meat-eating **theropod dinosaur**. Trace fossils such as this one preserve marks made by animals.

Trapped in amber

This **spider** got stuck in sticky tree sap millions of years ago. The sap hardened into rocklike amber, so every detail of the spider is preserved.

Body fossil

Most dinosaur fossils preserve parts of their bodies, such as this **Tyrannosaurus rex** skeleton. Usually, the bones are scattered, but sometimes they are joined together, as in life.

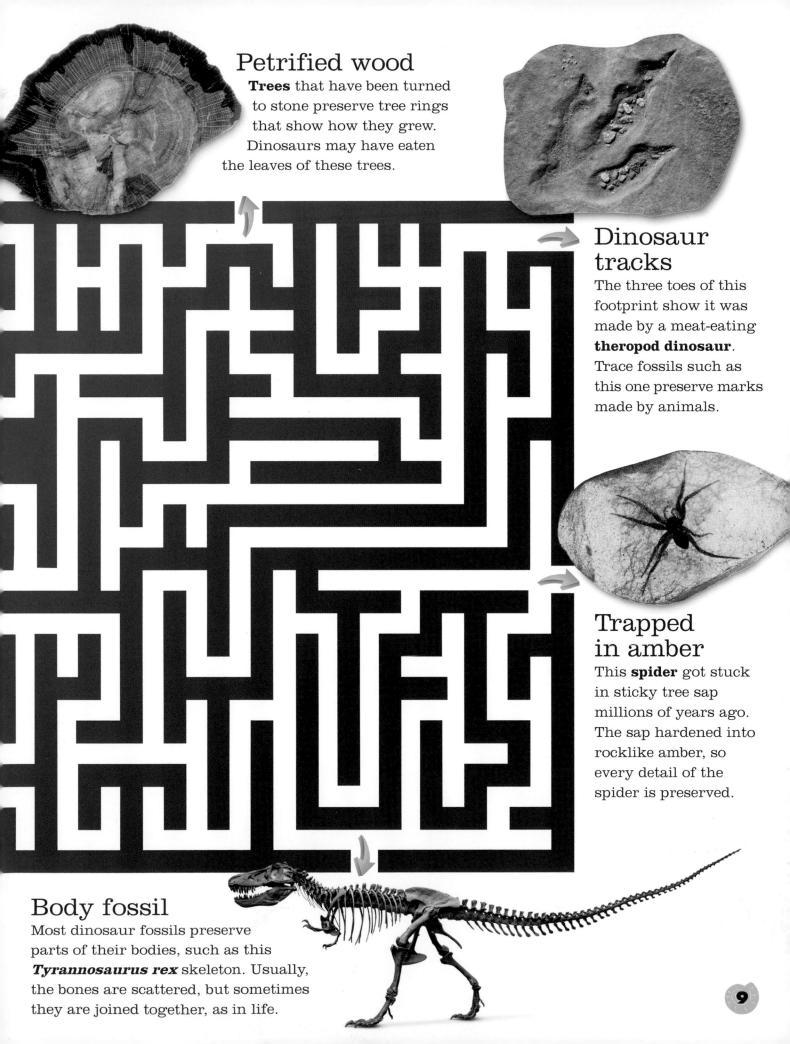

Fossil hunters

Dinosaur fossils survive for millions of years because they are sealed inside rocks. As rocks are worn away by the weather, they reveal the fossils hidden in them. Scientists make special expeditions to dig these out, sometimes finding evidence of dinosaurs that no one knew existed.

Discovery
In some parts of the world, rocks that date from the dinosaur age contain hundreds or even thousands of dinosaur fossils. These sites are famous, but many others are still hidden underground, waiting to be discovered by keen-eyed fossil hunters.

Recovery
Some fossils form in soft rock, making them easy to extract and clean up. Others have to be carefully cut out of hard rock. Fragile fossils are usually left attached to slabs of the rock that they are found in, and often strengthened with plaster before they are taken away.

Study
Back at the laboratory, scientists clean up fossils and examine them closely. They often recognize the species, but many fossils are new and exciting. Scientists sometimes use replicas of the bones to form the mounted skeletons seen in museums.

Dental drill

Chisels

Scraper

Ankylosaur fossil

Tools
Chipping fossils out of rocks can be slow, painstaking work, and can take many months to complete. Scientists use hammers and chisels at first, but they must eventually work with fine scrapers and brushes to make sure that they do not destroy the detail of a fossil.

Hammer

Brushes

Goggles

Gloves

Helmet

Reconstruction
Usually, some of the bones are missing, so scientists use their knowledge of similar animals to fill in the gaps. They can also figure out the position and size of the dinosaur's muscles. Eventually, they are able to build up a picture of what the dinosaur might have looked like.

11

DINOSAUR SCIENCE

Scientists have always tried to figure out what living, breathing dinosaurs might have been like. And now, thanks to new technologies and the recent discovery of amazingly detailed dinosaur fossils, they are finding out more than ever before.

Growth rings

Slicing through dinosaur bones reveals rings that show their age, with one ring standing for each year of life. These rings show that big dinosaurs such as *Apatosaurus* grew very fast.

Baby Apatosaurus   **Adult Apatosaurus**   **Human**

Anchiornis huxleyi

Color analysis

Some fossils may even preserve traces of color! Scientists who examined the fossil feathers of *Anchiornis huxleyi* under a very powerful microscope found possible evidence that this dinosaur had black-and-white wings and a rusty red crown.

Working replicas

Engineers can make mechanical replicas of dinosaurs to test theories about how they moved. Scientists use these to figure out how strong their muscles were—and even how powerfully the big hunters could bite.

Robotic Tyrannosaurus rex

Fuzzy, furlike feathers cover the body.

Sinosauropteryx fossil

The bones are made of strong metal.

Superfossils

Most of the truly exciting discoveries about dinosaurs are based on highly detailed fossils, found recently in places such as Liaoning in China. Fossils like this *Sinosauropteryx* preserve evidence of skin, feathers, and even the dinosaur's last meal.

Contents of stomach are preserved.

Computer modeling

Scientists use medical scanners to create 3-D computer images of dinosaur bones. They can use these images to build up skeletons and then animate them to show how dinosaurs moved.

Tyrannosaurus rex model

Shape of the legs shows whether it was a slow or fast runner.

Mesozoic Era

The first dinosaurs evolved about 230 million years ago, near the beginning of the Mesozoic Era. This vast span of time is divided into three periods—the Triassic, Jurassic, and Cretaceous—and ended in a catastrophic extinction 66 million years ago.

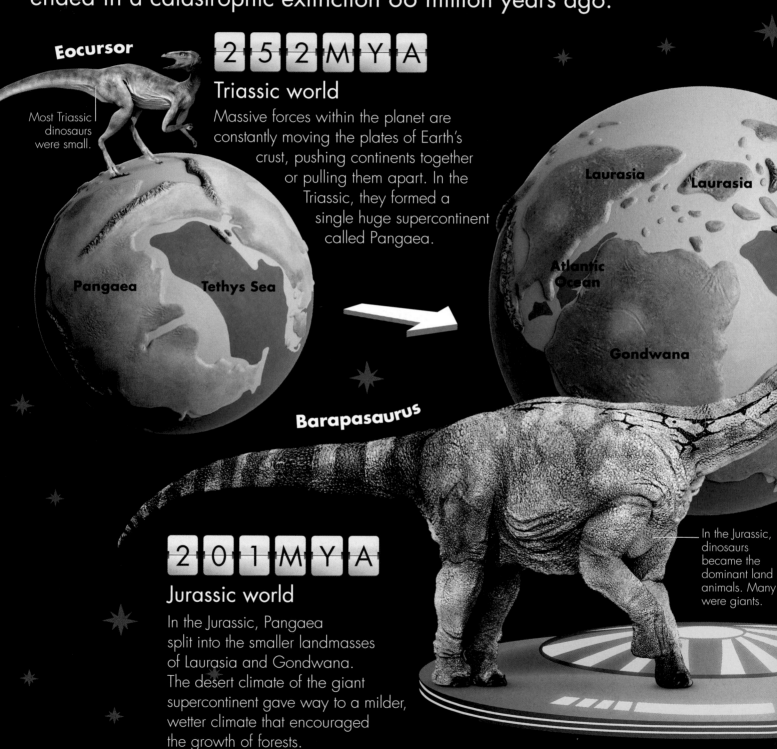

Eocursor

Most Triassic dinosaurs were small.

252 MYA

Triassic world

Massive forces within the planet are constantly moving the plates of Earth's crust, pushing continents together or pulling them apart. In the Triassic, they formed a single huge supercontinent called Pangaea.

Pangaea

Tethys Sea

Laurasia

Laurasia

Atlantic Ocean

Gondwana

Barapasaurus

In the Jurassic, dinosaurs became the dominant land animals. Many were giants.

201 MYA

Jurassic world

In the Jurassic, Pangaea split into the smaller landmasses of Laurasia and Gondwana. The desert climate of the giant supercontinent gave way to a milder, wetter climate that encouraged the growth of forests.

Mesozoic Earth had **warm climates**

Cretaceous world

During the Cretaceous, Laurasia and Gondwana broke up into smaller landmasses that were to turn into the continents we recognize today. Shallow seas covered many areas that later became dry land.

Alxasaurus

Dinosaurs evolved into a wide variety of forms in the Cretaceous.

Laurasia

Europe

North America

Asia

West Africa

India

Africa

South America

Tethys Sea

Australia

Antarctica

and **little or no ice** at the poles.

Back to the Mesozoic

Imagine you could travel back in time to the early part of the Mesozoic Era, more than 200 million years ago. You would find a world very different from ours, with no grass and no flowers. Life on land was dominated by huge reptiles, but there were also small mammals and insects much like the ones that live around us today.

PLANTS

INSECTS

MAMMALS

The early Mesozoic had only nonflowering trees and plants, such as this Pleuromeia, as well as cycads, conifers, mosses, and ferns. Flowering plants evolved in the Cretaceous Period, and grass had appeared by the end of the era.

Insects, such as this giant dragonfly, had evolved long before. But they flourished during the Mesozoic, evolving into most of the types we know now. They were important food for the smaller dinosaurs.

Only the size of a mouse, *Morganucodon* was typical of the small, furry mammals that chased after insects around the feet of the dinosaurs. They evolved at about the same time as the dinosaurs, but most stayed quite small until after the Mesozoic Era ended.

Paleozoic

542 MYA   400 MYA   300 MY

START   EJECT

Dazzling dinosaurs

After a slow start, the Mesozoic dinosaurs evolved into an amazing variety of forms. Scientists have found fossils of more than 800 different types, and there were probably at least ten times as many whose remains have not survived.

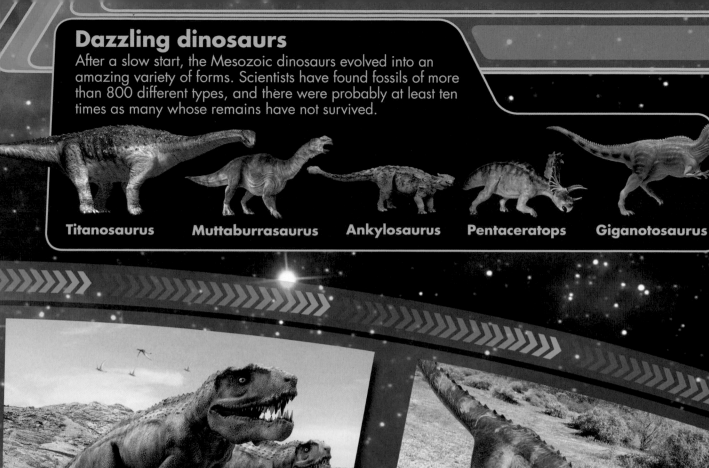

Titanosaurus   **Muttaburrasaurus**   **Ankylosaurus**   **Pentaceratops**   **Giganotosaurus**

REPTILES

DINOSAURS

When dinosaurs first appeared in the early Mesozoic, the biggest land animals were crocodiles and related reptiles such as *Postosuchus*—a massively built killer that probably preyed on early dinosaurs. But most of these other reptiles died out at the end of the Triassic Period, allowing the dinosaurs to take over.

The first dinosaurs were small, slender reptiles that ran around on two legs. One of the earliest to be found was the turkey-sized *Eoraptor*, which lived in South America about 230 million years ago, near the middle of the Triassic Period. Its sharp teeth and claws show that it was a hunter.

Mesozoic

Cenozoic

200 MYA   100 MYA   000 MYA

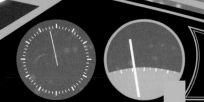

STOP

Beneath the waves

During the era when giant dinosaurs were roaming the land, similar creatures lived in the oceans. These marine reptiles were not closely related to dinosaurs, but many were just as big and spectacular, with massive jaws for seizing their prey.

Nothosaurus

This crocodile-like hunter lived on the shores of shallow seas during the middle and late Triassic Period, when the first dinosaurs were evolving on land. It had very long, sharp-pointed teeth, ideal for catching big, slippery fish.

Ichthyosaurus

Unlike *Nothosaurus*, the ichthyosaurs spent their entire lives in the sea, living and hunting like dolphins. *Ichthyosaurus* was a sleek, fast-swimming predator that preyed on fish, squid, and similar animals in early Jurassic oceans.

Elasmosaurus

Long-necked plesiosaurs such as *Elasmosaurus* had huge flippers, which they used like wings to "fly" in the water. These late Cretaceous marine reptiles gathered shellfish from the seabed, and caught fish and squid in open water.

The neck was as long as the rest of its body.

Kronosaurus

One group of plesiosaurs evolved into powerful predators called pliosaurs. They had short necks, huge jaws, and fearsome teeth. The late Cretaceous pliosaur *Kronosaurus* was one of the biggest at up to 30 ft (9 m) long.

Sharp, crocodile-like teeth made *Mosasaurus* a formidable hunter.

Mosasaurus

The mosasaurs appeared in the early Cretaceous Period and became dominant predators in the last 20 million years of the Mesozoic Era. Big ones such as *Mosasaurus* were powerful enough to kill other marine reptiles.

Hunters in the sky

Dinosaurs belonged to a group of **reptiles** called the **archosaurs**, which also included **crocodiles** and extinct flying reptiles called **pterosaurs**. These were agile, furry creatures, more like **enormous bats** than the slow-moving, scaly reptiles that we know today.

Rhamphorhynchus

Long finger bone

Rhamphorhynchus fossil

Although *Rhamphorhynchus* was from the late Jurassic, it had the **long tail** typical of early pterosaurs. This beautifully preserved **fossil skeleton** shows the very **short legs** folded forward under its small, lightweight body.

How pterosaurs evolved over time

The first pterosaurs appeared in the late Triassic. They were the size of crows, with short necks and long tails. Later types living in the Jurassic and Cretaceous had short tails, long necks, and crested heads with beaklike jaws. Some of these were airborne giants such as *Quetzalcoatlus*, which had wings the size of a small aircraft.

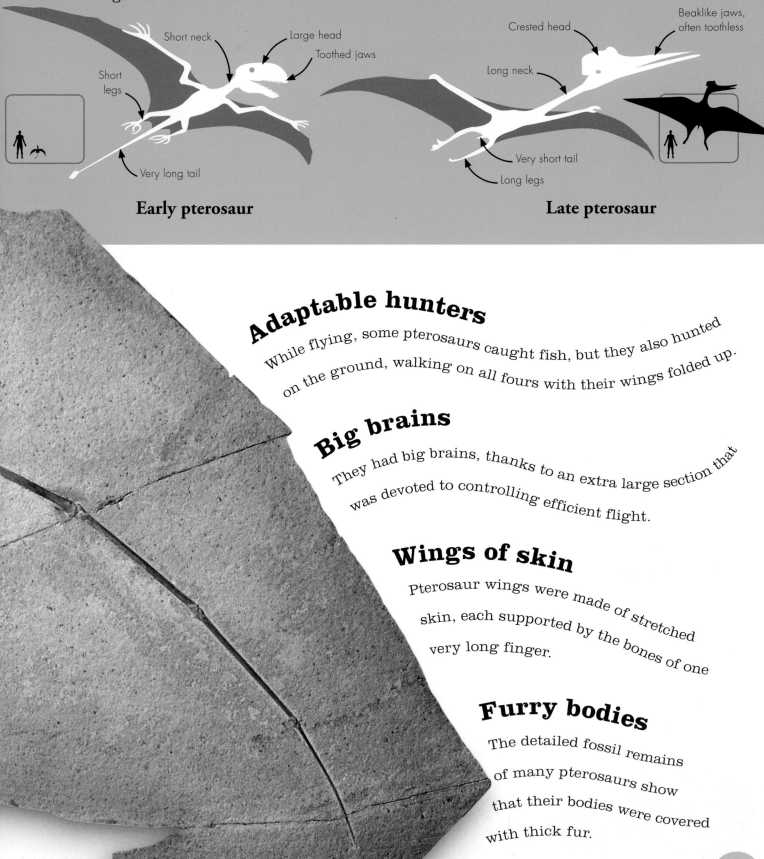

Short neck

Large head

Toothed jaws

Short legs

Very long tail

Early pterosaur

Crested head

Beaklike jaws, often toothless

Long neck

Very short tail

Long legs

Late pterosaur

Adaptable hunters

While flying, some pterosaurs caught fish, but they also hunted on the ground, walking on all fours with their wings folded up.

Big brains

They had big brains, thanks to an extra large section that was devoted to controlling efficient flight.

Wings of skin

Pterosaur wings were made of stretched skin, each supported by the bones of one very long finger.

Furry bodies

The detailed fossil remains of many pterosaurs show that their bodies were covered with thick fur.

SOARING PTEROSAURS

Pterosaurs were the most spectacular creatures to ever take to the skies. Some were huge, far bigger than any modern bird, and many had dramatic ornamental crests on their heads.

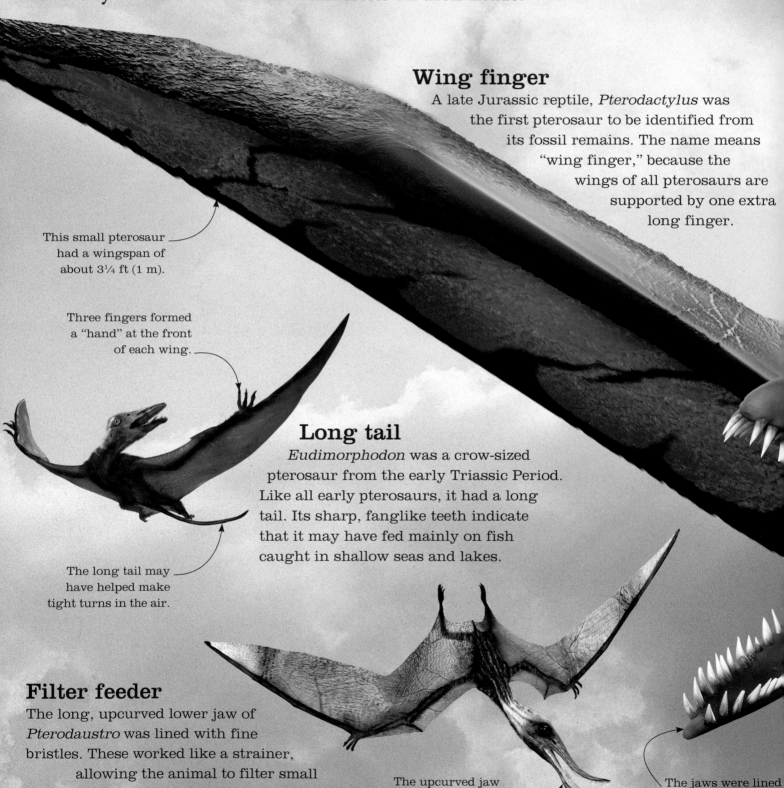

Wing finger

A late Jurassic reptile, *Pterodactylus* was the first pterosaur to be identified from its fossil remains. The name means "wing finger," because the wings of all pterosaurs are supported by one extra long finger.

This small pterosaur had a wingspan of about 3¼ ft (1 m).

Three fingers formed a "hand" at the front of each wing.

Long tail

Eudimorphodon was a crow-sized pterosaur from the early Triassic Period. Like all early pterosaurs, it had a long tail. Its sharp, fanglike teeth indicate that it may have fed mainly on fish caught in shallow seas and lakes.

The long tail may have helped make tight turns in the air.

Filter feeder

The long, upcurved lower jaw of *Pterodaustro* was lined with fine bristles. These worked like a strainer, allowing the animal to filter small creatures from the water in much the same way as a modern flamingo.

The upcurved jaw was ideal for sifting surface water.

The jaws were lined with sharp teeth for catching fish.

Although big, the
crest was very light.

Colorful crest

The magnificent *Tupandactylus* lived in what
is now Brazil in the early Cretaceous Period.
Its head was crowned with an enormous crest
made of the same material as a bird's beak.
The crest was supported by two bony rods.

Many males had
long, showy crests
on their heads.

Slender wings were
ideal for soaring
on oceanic winds.

Toothless giant

A late Cretaceous flying reptile,
Pteranodon was one of the
biggest pterosaurs, with a
wingspan of up to 20 ft (6 m).
It had a long, toothless beak
and probably hunted fish at
sea like a modern albatross.

Dinosaur family tree

Dinosaurs belonged to the **same group of reptiles** as the pterosaurs, but started evolving separately early in the **Triassic Period**. In the late Triassic, they were divided into **two basic types**, ornithischians and saurischians, which then split into the **five main dinosaur groups**.

ORNITHOPODS
Ornithopods were among the most successful dinosaurs. They were plant-eaters that mainly walked on their hind legs like the meat-eating theropods. Big ornithopods such as *Camptosaurus* sometimes walked on all fours.

Styracosaurus

MARGINOCEPHALIANS
These were made up of two groups of plant-eaters: the thick-skulled pachycephalosaurs and the ceratopsians, such as *Styracosaurus*, with their horned faces and elaborate neck frills.

THYREOPHORANS
The heavily armored thyreophorans were an early group of ornithischians. They included the stegosaurs, which had rows of plates and spines on their backs, and tanklike ankylosaurs such as *Edmontonia*.

ORNITHISCHIANS
The ornithischians were all plant-eaters with relatively short necks. They had beaks for cropping vegetation, as well as teeth. Their pelvic or hip bones resembled those of modern birds, even though they are not closely related.

Edmontonia

Bird-hipped

More than **1,000** species of dinosaurs lived in the Mesozoic

Apatosaurus

SAUROPODOMORPHS
This group of dinosaurs included all the real giants. They were heavily built plant-eaters that supported their immense weight on all four legs. Most of them had very long necks, and many had equally long tails.

Camptosaurus

Iberomesornis

BIRDS
The theropod group that includes dinosaurs such as *Deinonychus* also gave rise to the birds, which are still living around us today.

SAURISCHIANS
The saurischian dinosaurs had longer necks than the ornithischians. Some were plant-eaters called sauropodomorphs, but others known as theropods were meat-eating hunters. Typical saurischians had pelvic bones like those of lizards.

THEROPODS
Nearly all theropods were predators—meat-eaters that preyed on other animals. They all ran on their hind legs. Some were heavily armed giants with massive jaws, but others were more like modern birds.

Deinonychus

Lizard-hipped

Era. Some were the LARGEST animals ever to walk the Earth.

Naming dinosaurs

Scientists name dinosaurs based on Latin or Greek words. All animals have scientific names. Some species share first names: A tiger is *Panthera tigris* and a lion is *Panthera leo*. Both these big cats are called *Panthera* because they are closely related. Dinosaur names use exactly the same system.

PSITTACOSAURUS

SIT-uh-kuh-SORE-us

This dinosaur had a beak like that of a parrot. Its name is derived from the word *psittacine* (the name of a group of birds that includes parrots) and *saurus* (the Greek word for lizard). So *Psittacosaurus* means "**parrot lizard**."

VELOCIRAPTOR

vuh-LOSS-uh-RAP-tur

The bones of this dinosaur show that it was a fast-running hunter. Its name means "**speedy thief**." As with tigers and lions, the first name covers two species—*Velociraptor mongoliensis* and *Velociraptor osmolskae*.

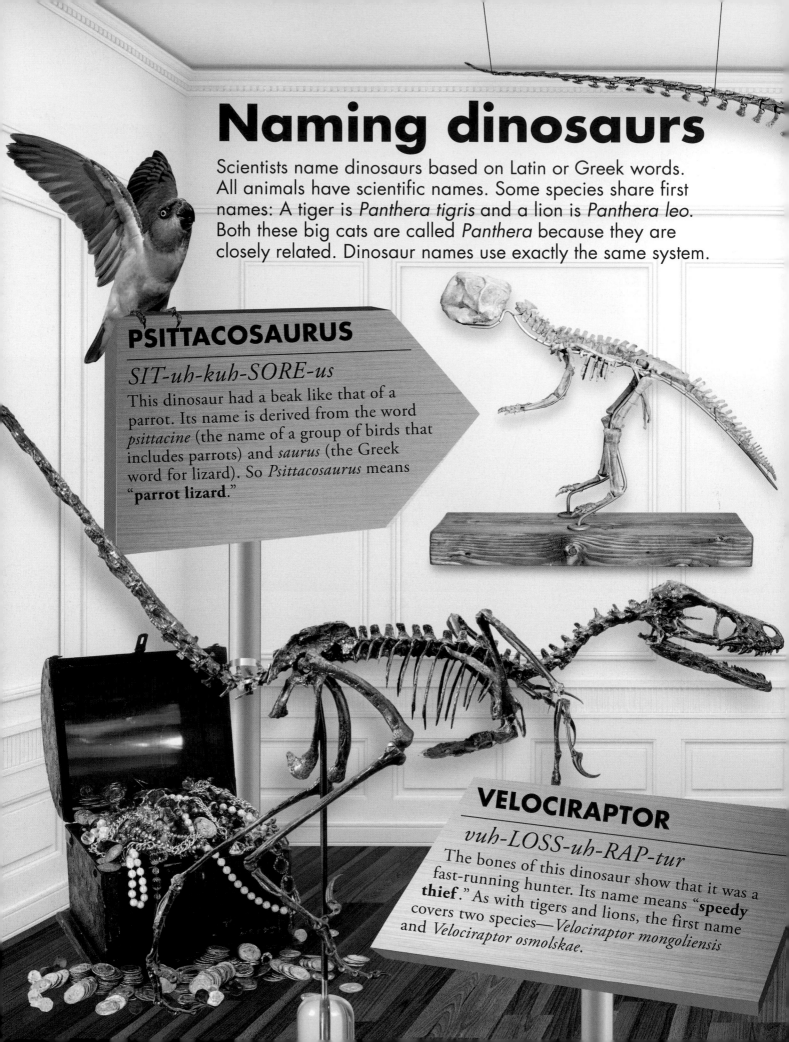

ORNITHOMIMUS

OR-nith-oh-MY-mus

The slender build, long legs, and beaky face of this dinosaur reminded scientists of the ostrich and similar fast-running birds. So they called it *Ornithomimus*—Greek for **"bird mimic"**—despite the fact that it couldn't fly.

TRICERATOPS

try-SAIR-uh-tops

The obvious features of this dinosaur's skull are two long horns on its brow and a third on its nose. These features earned it the name *Triceratops*, which combines three Greek words meaning **"three-horned face."**

Inside a hunter

The heavily armed **Tyrannosaurus rex** was one of the biggest theropods—a group of dinosaurs that were nearly all meat-eaters. This hunter had many specialized features, such as huge jaws and teeth.

Massive **neck muscles** held up the heavy head and jaws.

Inside out

The fossils of dinosaurs preserve only their bones and teeth, and sometimes skin and feathers. But scientists have been able to figure out what dinosaur muscles were like, and even how they digested their food.

A powerful **heart** pumped blood up the very long neck.

Very short **arms**, each with two sharply clawed fingers.

The huge body contained a big **stomach** and long **intestine**.

Under a plant-eater's skin

Long-necked sauropods such as **Brachiosaurus** specialized in gathering leaves from the tops of tall trees. Their bulky bodies were ideally adapted for their leafy diet.

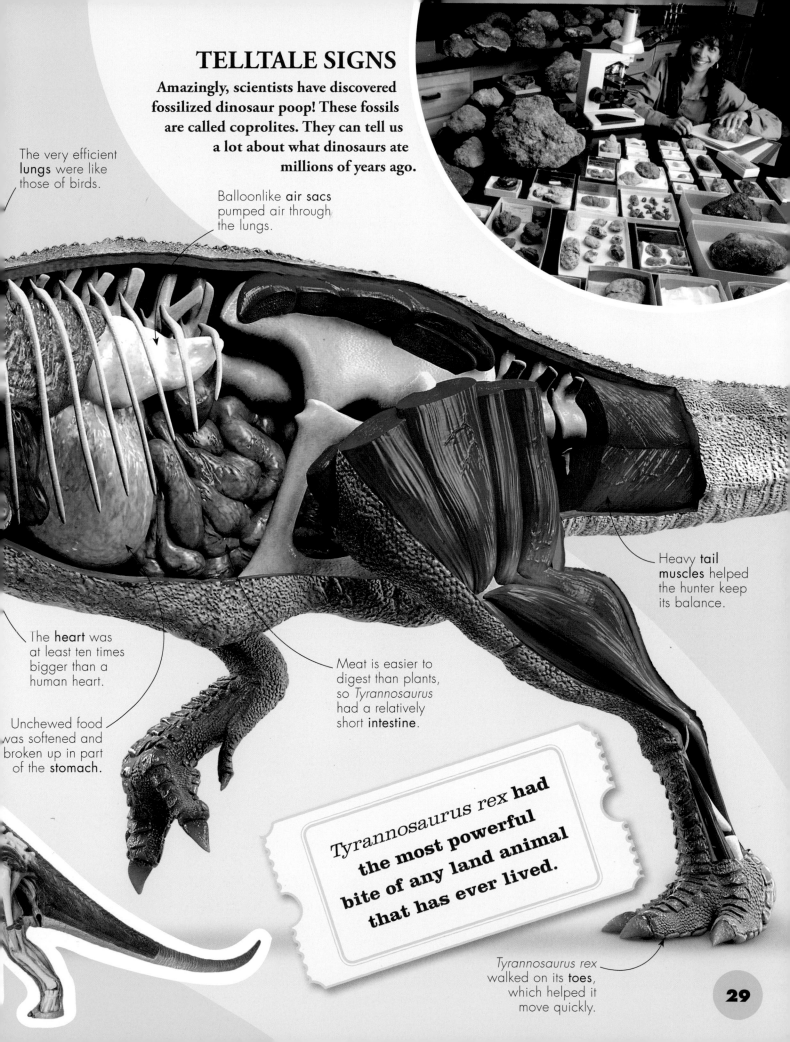

TELLTALE SIGNS

Amazingly, scientists have discovered fossilized dinosaur poop! These fossils are called coprolites. They can tell us a lot about what dinosaurs ate millions of years ago.

The very efficient **lungs** were like those of birds.

Balloonlike **air sacs** pumped air through the lungs.

Heavy **tail muscles** helped the hunter keep its balance.

The **heart** was at least ten times bigger than a human heart.

Meat is easier to digest than plants, so *Tyrannosaurus* had a relatively short **intestine**.

Unchewed food was softened and broken up in part of the **stomach**.

Tyrannosaurus rex had the most powerful bite of any land animal that has ever lived.

Tyrannosaurus rex walked on its **toes**, which helped it move quickly.

SUPER SENSES

Whether they are predators or prey, animals need acute senses to survive. Fossil evidence, such as well-developed ear bones and large eye sockets, shows that dinosaurs were no exception.

Eye sockets angled forward

Nostrils picked up the scent of prey

Prey animals need sharp senses to **detect danger** and survive.

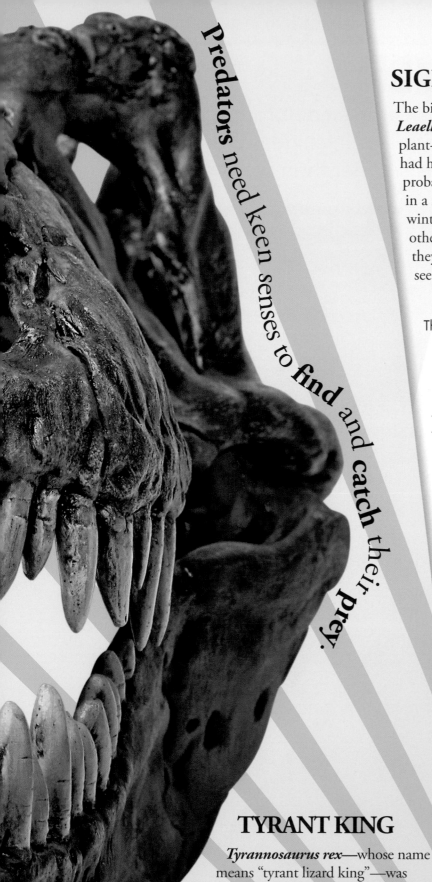

SIGHT

Big eyes saw well in dim light

The big eye sockets of **Leaellynasaura**, a small plant-eater, show that it had huge eyes. These were probably an adaptation to life in a region that had very dark winters. Scientists think that many other dinosaurs had good eyesight because they needed to see at night, and also to see the crest colors of other dinosaurs.

The tall bony crest was hollow

HEARING

Some duck-billed dinosaurs such as **Lambeosaurus** had cavities in their skulls that seem to have made their calls louder, like trumpets. This means that sound was important to them and suggests that they had good hearing. Hunters would also need good ears to detect noises made by prey.

A good sense of smell was vital

TYRANT KING

Tyrannosaurus rex—whose name means "tyrant lizard king"—was a ferocious hunter. The shape of its brain shows that it had an acute sense of smell and very sharp sight for finding prey. Its eye sockets also show that the eyes pointed forward, like those of most hunters. This helped it judge the distance of its target accurately.

SMELL

Some hunters would have relied on their sensitive noses to sniff out their prey. The long snout of **Utahraptor**, for example, indicates that it had an acute sense of smell. Many hunters would also have eaten rotting meat, tracking it down by the smell of decay drifting through the air.

BRAINPOWER

Many dinosaurs had astonishingly small brains compared to their gigantic size. Most were less intelligent than crocodiles, for example, but a few were smarter than we used to think.

TROODON
THE QUIZMASTER

Kentrosaurus was as big as a bull, but its brain was not much bigger than a walnut shell.

Troodon

If dinosaurs took part in a quiz, this lightweight hunter would be the quizmaster. Its brain was bigger than we would expect for a dinosaur of its size, so it must have been quite intelligent. This would have helped it figure out how to catch its prey.

Kentrosaurus

This spiky dinosaur was a stegosaur—a group of plant-eaters that had tiny brains compared to their massive bodies. *Kentrosaurus* could not have been very clever, but since its food was easy to find, it didn't need to be.

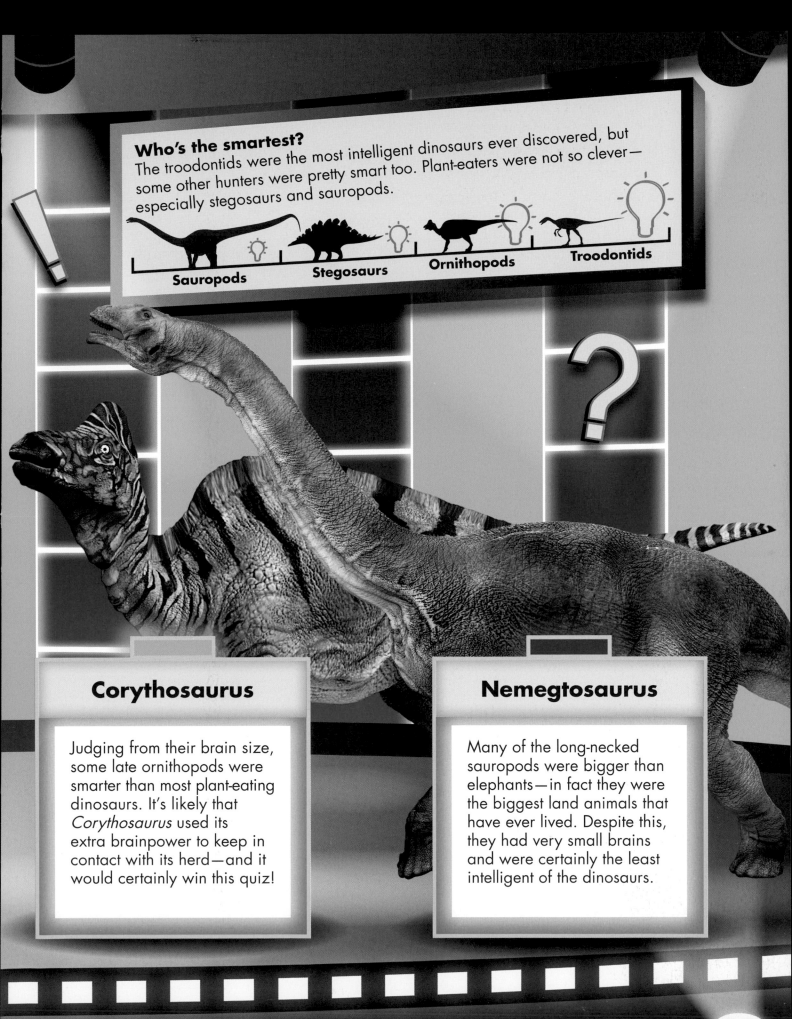

Who's the smartest?
The troodontids were the most intelligent dinosaurs ever discovered, but some other hunters were pretty smart too. Plant-eaters were not so clever—especially stegosaurs and sauropods.

Sauropods **Stegosaurs** **Ornithopods** **Troodontids**

Corythosaurus

Judging from their brain size, some late ornithopods were smarter than most plant-eating dinosaurs. It's likely that *Corythosaurus* used its extra brainpower to keep in contact with its herd—and it would certainly win this quiz!

Nemegtosaurus

Many of the long-necked sauropods were bigger than elephants—in fact they were the biggest land animals that have ever lived. Despite this, they had very small brains and were certainly the least intelligent of the dinosaurs.

ULTIMATE PREDATORS

The most powerful hunters that ever stalked the Earth belonged to a group of dinosaurs known as theropods. They included large and fearsome creatures like *Tyrannosaurus rex*, but many theropods were much smaller, lighter, and quicker on their feet.

COELOPHYSIS

KEY FEATURE: LIGHTWEIGHT HUNTER

Date: 221–201 MYA (Triassic)

Size: 10 ft (3 m) long

Fossil location: USA, Africa, and China

The lightly built *Coelophysis* was one of the earliest theropods, but it had all the key features of the group, such as strong hind legs, a long neck, and a mouthful of sharp, bladelike teeth.

ALLOSAURUS

KEY FEATURE: SLASHING TEETH

Date: 150–145 MYA (late Jurassic)

Size: 39 ft (12 m) long

Fossil location: USA and Portugal

The big plant-eating dinosaurs of the late Jurassic were preyed on by giants such as *Allosaurus*, which used its saw-edged teeth to slash at its victims and inflict lethal wounds.

COMPSOGNATHUS

KEY FEATURE: SMALL AND AGILE

Date: 151–145 MYA (late Jurassic)

Size: 3¼ ft (1 m) long

Fossil location: Germany and France

The turkey-sized *Compsognathus* was an agile hunter that would have chased after small animals such as lizards and insects. Its body was covered with fuzzy, hairlike feathers.

DEINONYCHUS

KEY FEATURE: KILLER CLAWS

Date: 120–112 MYA (early Cretaceous)

Size: 13 ft (4 m) long

Fossil location: USA

A ferocious hunter, *Deinonychus* was armed with a long, sharp killer claw on each foot that it could use to stab and rip at its victims. It also had grasping claws on its long, powerful arms.

SPINOSAURUS

KEY FEATURE: CROCODILE-LIKE JAWS

Date: 100–95 MYA (mid Cretaceous)

Size: 52½ ft (16 m) long

Fossil location: Morocco, Libya, and Egypt

One of the biggest theropods, this giant hunter had a tall crest running the length of its back. It used its crocodile-like teeth to seize and eat big fish, as well as other dinosaurs.

TROODON

KEY FEATURE: LARGE BRAIN

Date: 77–67 MYA (late Cretaceous)

Size: 8 ft (2.4 m) long

Fossil location: USA and Canada

Troodon and its relatives had big brains compared to their size, which would have helped them outwit their prey. But the shape of their teeth suggests that they may have also eaten plants.

TYRANNOSAURUS REX

KEY FEATURE: BONE-CRUSHING JAWS

Date: 70–66 MYA (late Cretaceous)

Size: 39 ft (12 m) long

Fossil location: USA and Canada

Armed with huge, strong teeth and powerful jaws, this massively built hunter could bite straight through the bones of its victims. Only one species of Tyrannosaurus is known—*Tyrannosaurus rex*.

ODD THEROPODS

Theropods were typically heavily armed hunters, but some were very different. Several chased after insects, and a few preferred to eat plants. Many had feathers, and one group—the birds—even developed the ability to fly.

Ostrich dinosaur

Some theropods were slender, with slim hind legs and long necks. They had small, beaky heads with tiny teeth or no teeth at all. These superfast dinosaurs looked like ostriches and probably had a similar way of life, feeding on leaves, seeds, and small animals.

Struthiomimus

Like most dinosaurs, Struthiomimus has a Latin name, which means "ostrich mimic."

With its long, powerful legs, *Struthiomimus* was built for speed.

The arms were short but very powerful.

Shuvuuia

Ant-eater?

The chicken-sized **Shuvuuia** looked like a miniature ostrich dinosaur with very short arms. It had just one working finger on each hand, but it had a very strong claw that might have been useful for ripping into the nests of ants and termites.

Citipati had a bony crest on its head.

Citipati

Egg thief

With its beak and long, feathered arms, *Citipati* looked even more birdlike than the ostrich dinosaurs. Its diet may have included eggs stolen from the nests of other dinosaurs.

Therizinosaurus

The long feathers on this animal's arms were mainly for show.

Therizinosaurus was tall enough to reach into treetops.

Plant-lover

This was the strangest of the theropods because it seems to have given up eating meat. Its small, leaf-shaped teeth and unusually large digestive system suggests that it fed mainly on plants.

Archaeopteryx

Small flight muscles made **Archaeopteryx** a weak flier.

Early bird

Many small theropods had long arms with ornamental feathers. A few used them to glide between trees. Eventually, animals such as the late Jurassic **Archaeopteryx** were able to fly.

Escaping the enemy

With huge, hungry, heavily armed hunters on the prowl, other dinosaurs needed ways to protect themselves. They could run, hide, back each other up, or fight back!

Dinosaurs with long tails may have lashed them like whips.

Quick getaway

Small, light dinosaurs such as **Othnielosaurus** could rely on their speed and agility to escape from enemies. Bigger hunters were just as fast, but they may not have been quite as agile. Modern cheetahs chasing after small, nimble gazelles often have the same problem.

The long, slender back legs were built for speed.

Camouflage

We do not know what color dinosaurs were, but it is likely that many small species were camouflaged. Dull browns and dappled patterns on the skin would have made them difficult to spot for hunters, especially in thick undergrowth or shady forests.

Fighting back

A few of the bigger plant-eaters were armed with weapons that would have made them dangerous prey. Stegosaurs such as this **Huayangosaurus** had sharp spikes on their tails that could cripple enemies. The smashed bones of some hunters show the damage these dinosaurs could do.

The sharp spikes were backed up by powerful tail muscles.

Lying low

Some small dinosaurs such as **Oryctodromeus** seem to have dug burrows in the ground. They could have hidden in these burrows to stay out of sight of predators. They could also dive in if they sensed danger, just as rabbits do when they fear an attack.

Safety in numbers

Fossilized footprints of plant-eating dinosaurs indicate that some may have lived in herds. This would have been safer than living alone, because while some fed, the rest could watch for danger. The herd could also jointly drive enemies away, especially if they were armed with sharp horns like these **Centrosaurus**.

BATTLE ROYAL

BONE-CRUNCHING JAWS

VS.

COLOSSAL CLAWS

THE THERIZINOSAURUS

Its incredibly long, sharp claws, shaped like curved sword blades, must have made this tall plant-eater a very dangerous target. It could have killed an enemy such as *Tarbosaurus* with a single well-aimed stab.

OMNIVORE

★★★★★★★★★★★★
HEIGHT   LENGTH
★★★★★★★★★★★★
20 ft [6 m]   36 ft [11 m]
★★★★★★★★★★★★

5 tons

TARBOSAURUS

This massively built tyrannosaur could use its strong jaws and teeth to bite clean through the bones of its victims. Like *Therizinosaurus*, it lived in Asia near the end of the Mesozoic Era.

CARNIVORE

★★★★★★★★★★★★
HEIGHT   LENGTH
★★★★★★★★★★★★
13 ft [4 m]   36 ft [11 m]
★★★★★★★★★★★★

5 tons

A FIGHT NOT TO BE MISSED!

Ready, set... go!

Many two-legged dinosaurs were quick on their feet. We know this because their skeletons, and the muscles attached to them, are like those of fast-running birds such as ostriches. Even big, heavy dinosaurs were probably as active as modern elephants.

Super sprinter

One of the fastest-running dinosaurs, *Gallimimus* was built like a modern ostrich. Its long, slim legs had massive thigh muscles that would have given it the speed it needed to escape from the fearsome tyrannosaurs that were its biggest enemies.

High and mighty

Heavy, long-necked sauropods such as *Barosaurus* walked on four pillarlike legs like elephants. But they held their heads and tails high, and probably stood up on their back legs to reach high up into trees.

Athletic hunter

Most predators have to be fast to catch their prey. The leg bones and muscles of dinosaur hunters such as this *Allosaurus* show that they were certainly able to run, although the smaller, lighter ones probably ran faster than the giants.

Speedy plant-eater

Today, many of the fastest animals are plant-eaters like gazelles that need to escape from meat-eating enemies. Many small plant-eating dinosaurs such as *Lesothosaurus* could move fast for exactly the same reason—to get out of trouble.

Browsing giants

The **biggest and heaviest** animals to walk the Earth were the spectacular sauropods—**long-necked plant-eaters** that **gathered leaves from tall trees**. They had **huge stomachs** for digesting vast amounts of plant food, and supported their weight on **massive tree-trunk legs**.

PLATEOSAURUS
This was one of the earliest of the long-necked plant-eaters. It stood on its hind legs to reach into the treetops, and may have used its long-toed front feet like hands to gather food.

92 ft
[28 m]
LONG

26 ft
[8 m]
LONG

23 ft
[7 m]
LONG

VULCANODON
This early Jurassic sauropod was named *Vulcanodon* because its fossils were found beneath a layer of ancient volcanic lava. It was much smaller than the earth-shaking giants that evolved later on.

BRACHIOSAURUS

One of the heavyweight champions of the Jurassic world, *Brachiosaurus* weighed as much as six elephants. Its long front legs gave it immense height, like an outsized giraffe, so it could feed much higher than other dinosaurs.

BAROSAURUS

The incredibly long neck of this late Jurassic sauropod allowed it to browse high in the trees. It used the peglike teeth at the front of its jaws to comb through the foliage, stripping all the leaves from the twigs.

DICRAEOSAURUS

Unlike most of its kind, *Dicraeosaurus* had a very short neck and seems to have eaten the leaves of low-growing trees and bushes. Its backbone had tall, bony spines that may have supported an impressive spiky crest.

75 ft

[23 m]

LONG

39 ft

[12 m]

LONG

39 ft

[12 m]

LONG

SALTASAURUS

Many of the giant sauropods lived during the Jurassic Period, but one group, the titanosaurs, survived until the end of the dinosaur era. *Saltasaurus*, one of the last, had an armor of bony studs on its skin.

LITTLE and **LARGE**

We usually think of dinosaurs as colossal animals, often with terrifying teeth and claws. But many of the dinosaurs that ran around the feet of these giants were no bigger than chickens, and others were much smaller.

Argentinosaurus

This titanosaur was a true giant, and possibly the largest land animal that has ever lived. At 97 tons, it weighed as much as 13 elephants! We are still not sure how it managed to walk around without collapsing under its own weight.

Anchiornis

This late Jurassic feathered hunter is one of the smallest known Mesozoic dinosaurs. At only 4 oz (110 g), it weighed far less than a crow. Small, lightweight dinosaurs like this one were probably very common.

Anchiornis
14 in (35 cm) long

Herrerasaurus
20 ft (6 m) long

Argentinosaurus
98 ft (30 m) long

Smallest living
DINOSAUR

Since scientists agree that birds are dinosaurs, the smallest living bird—the Cuban bee hummingbird—is also the smallest living dinosaur. At under $\frac{7}{100}$ oz (2 g), it weighs less than some beetles!

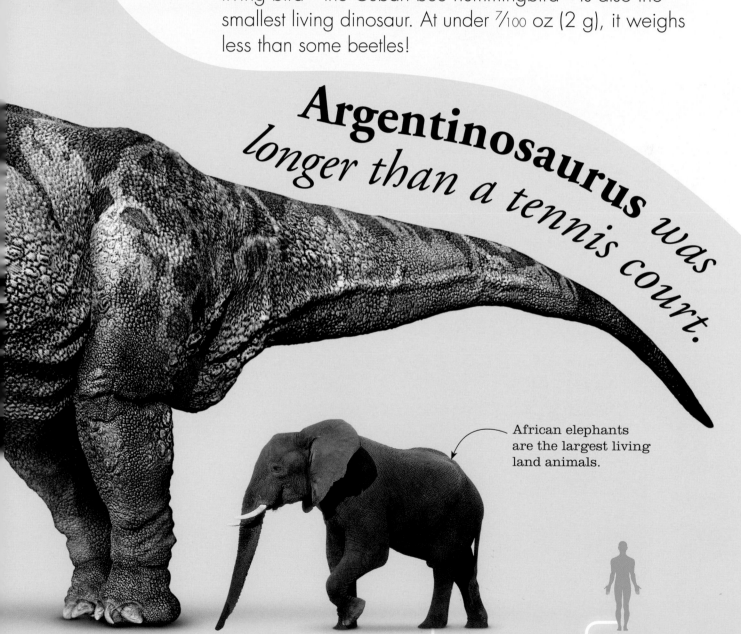

Argentinosaurus was longer than a tennis court.

African elephants are the largest living land animals.

African elephant	Human
11 ft (3.5 m) long	6 ft (1.8 m) tall

47

PLATED STEGOSAURS

The Jurassic forests were home to spectacular stegosaurs—a group of heavily built plant-eaters with rows of big, bony plates and spikes running down their backs. The plates may have been used for display, while the tail spikes served as weapons.

The supersized plates were not attached to the backbone.

Stegosaurus

The biggest and most well-known stegosaur, this one grew to 30 ft (9 m) long. The huge plates on its back made it look spectacular. They may have been used to impress rival stegosaurs rather than scare enemies.

Tall, triangular back plates

The oval, bony plates were covered with tough keratin—the material that makes up your fingernails.

Kentrosaurus

With a name meaning "sharp-point lizard," *Kentrosaurus* had long, pointed spikes on its lower back, where some stegosaurs had plates. The spikes would have made it a dangerous target for hungry meat-eaters.

Long spikes

Sharp shoulder spikes helped deter enemies.

Tuojiangosaurus

Named after the place in China where its fossils were found, *Tuojiangosaurus* and Tuojiang shoulder and it also was armed with formidable spikes. Like many stegosaurs, it also had bony plates along its back and hips. tail spikes along its back and hips.

Stegosaur ancestor

Stegosaurs and ankylosaurs belonged to a group of dinosaurs called the thyreophorans. Both evolved from animals like this early Jurassic *Scelidosaurus*. Its back was armored with bony studs, which evolved into plates and spikes in stegosaurs.

Long hind legs

ARMORED ANKYLOSAURS

The massive, tanklike ankylosaurs were plant-eaters that walked on all fours and had surprisingly tiny brains. Without their tough, bony body armor, they would have been easy targets for predators. Some ankylosaurs had spectacular spines as well as armor, and others fought off their enemies with bone-shattering tail clubs.

Horns projected from head and cheeks

GARGOYLEOSAURUS

One of the smallest and earliest known ankylosaurs, this dinosaur lived in the late Jurassic and grew to 13 ft (4 m). Its head and body were studded with horns and long spines.

The tail club was made of solid bone

GASTONIA

Like nearly all other ankylosaurs, *Gastonia* had small, leaf-shaped teeth, and probably did not chew its food. Its back was covered with bladelike spikes, deterring all but the most hungry predators.

Sideways pointing spikes

SAUROPELTA

This spectacular animal lived in what is now North America in the early Cretaceous. Its back was protected by a sheet of tooth-breaking bony plates, but the huge spines were probably partly for show.

Massive spines jutted out of its shoulders

Bony plates covered the whole body

ANKYLOSAURUS

The massive tail club of this late Cretaceous giant evolved as a weapon for fighting off the biggest of all land predators—the tyrannosaurs. It was the biggest ankylosaur, growing up to 20 ft (6 m), with some of the toughest armor.

EUOPLOCEPHALUS

Like *Ankylosaurus*, this broad-bodied heavyweight could defend itself by swinging its heavy tail club at the legs of its enemies. With its thick armor, it weighed as much as a big rhinoceros.

Even the eyes had armored eyelids

Toothy tales

We can figure out what dinosaurs ate by looking at their teeth—as well as their beaks, if they had them. We can even tell how they collected their food, and if they chewed it to a pulp before swallowing it.

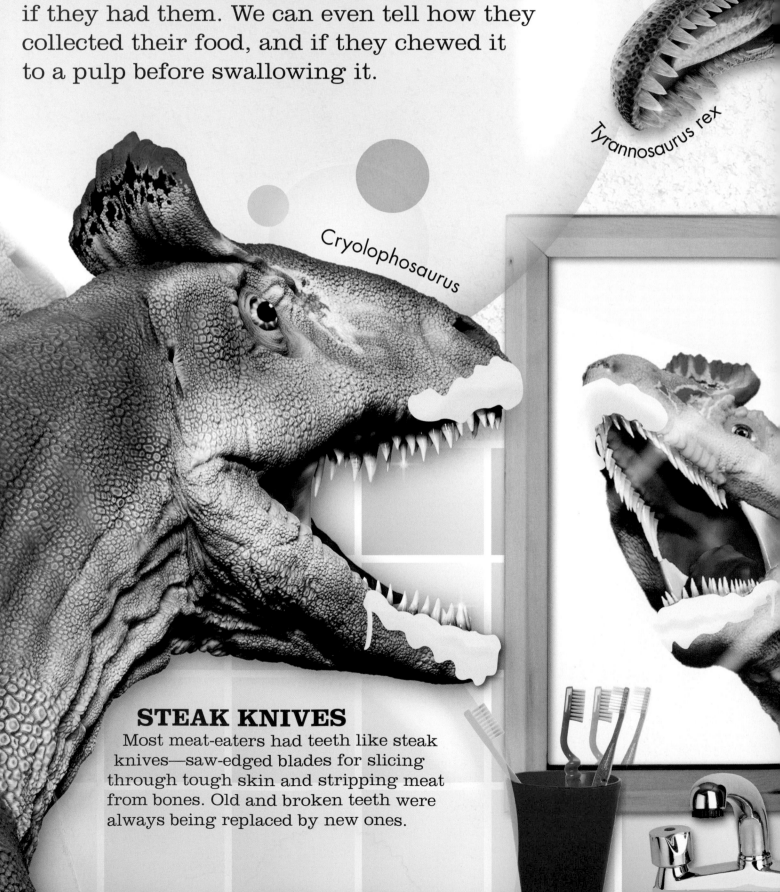

Tyrannosaurus rex

Cryolophosaurus

STEAK KNIVES

Most meat-eaters had teeth like steak knives—saw-edged blades for slicing through tough skin and stripping meat from bones. Old and broken teeth were always being replaced by new ones.

BONE-CRUSHERS

The massively powerful tyrannosaurs had equally massive teeth. These huge, sharp spikes, far stronger than the teeth of most meat-eaters, were able to bite through solid bone.

Tyrannosaurus rex had up to 58 huge teeth—the biggest were about 8 in (20 cm) long.

Barosaurus

LEAF COMBS

Some long-necked leaf-eaters had rows of teeth shaped like pencil stubs. Scientists think these dinosaurs used their teeth to comb through twigs and strip off leaves before swallowing them whole.

Edmontosaurus

The ducklike bill was backed up by rows of cheek teeth for chewing tough plants.

TOUGH BEAKS

All plant-eating ornithischian dinosaurs had sharp-edged beaks on the tips of their snouts for gathering plants. Many, such as this *Edmontosaurus*, chewed the plants to a pulp using highly specialized teeth.

53

ON THE MENU

TASTY SNACKS

A few dinosaurs were omnivores—they liked to eat a variety of things, provided they had high nutritional value. *Heterodontosaurus* had several types of teeth to cope with its mixed diet.

- Tender shoots
- Juicy roots
- Crunchy insects
- Lizards

Heterodontosaurus

FRESH SALAD

Beaked plant-eaters such as *Scelidosaurus* fed on low-growing plants that they could reach easily. They probably chose young, tender plants that were easy to chew and digest.

- Tender leaves
- Green shoots
- Ferns
- Mosses

Scelidosaurus

Barapasaurus

RAW GREENS

The very long necks of big sauropods gave them the ability to reach into the treetops to gather leaves. They swallowed them whole and did not choose them very carefully.

- Conifer leaves
- Cycad fronds
- Tree ferns
- Mosses

Different types of dinosaurs enjoyed different types of food. Some would eat almost anything, just like us. Others were hunters that preyed on other animals, including dinosaurs. Many just ate plants, and often had to gather huge amounts to feed their big bodies.

MEAT COURSE

Most of the theropod dinosaurs were hunters that attacked and ate other animals. Big ones like **Giganotosaurus** used their deadly teeth to kill other dinosaurs.

- Giant plant-eaters
- Smaller meat-eaters
- Dead animals

Giganotosaurus

DID THEY SWALLOW STONES?

Some birds swallow stones to grind up the food in their stomachs. A few dinosaurs may have done the same.

FISH DINNER

Suchomimus and its close relatives had teeth like those of crocodiles and used them to catch fish. But they also ate any other animals that they could catch.

- Big fish
- Small dinosaurs
- Small pterosaurs

Suchomimus

BONEHEADS

The pachycephalosaurs are some of the most puzzling of all dinosaurs. The tops of their heads were incredibly strong, made of bone up to 10 in (25 cm) thick. Scientists are still trying to understand why they needed such strong skulls.

PACHYCEPHALOSAURUS

FOSSIL FINDS
North America

DATE
70–65 MYA

DIET
Omnivore

Superstrong skull

This *Stegoceras* skull shows how the part of the skull covering the brain—the cranium—was thickened to form a massive dome. It's possible that this was for protection when rival males butted each other head-to-head, just as wild sheep do today when fighting for status. But some scientists think these dinosaurs may have rammed each other in the sides instead.

SIZE: 23 ft (7 m) long

Big-headed

Pachycephalosaurus was the biggest of the boneheads—its head alone was about 31 in (80 cm) long and crowned with a ring of spikes. Like other pachycephalosaurs, it had several different types of teeth in its jaws. This suggests that it was an omnivore—an animal that eats many different kinds of food.

TOP MALE

Like many modern animals, dinosaurs may have fought each other over status, territory, or breeding partners. Today, most of these combats involve rival males. Dinosaurs probably behaved in the same way.

DAWN PATROL

During the breeding season, a mature male *Zuniceratops* patrols his territory. He finds signs that a rival *Zuniceratops* has moved onto his patch. He worries that the rival male could lure away the females that form his family.

FIGHT

Roaring and pawing the ground, the rivals lock horns. The intruder is very strong, but the other male is on his home turf and won't give up easily.

I think I'm stronger than the guy who lives here, but he looks very sure of himself!

INTRUDER

With a bellow, the other male suddenly appears in full view. He is younger and stronger than the resident male, and struts around, showing off his long horns and dramatic neck frill. The other male does the same, and they size each other up. If one feels weaker, he will run away rather than risk a fight!

VICTORY

The intruder is not very confident and makes a mistake. His rival knocks him flat, and proclaims his win with a loud bellow. He is the top male!

59

Crests and frills

Many dinosaurs had dramatic horns, crests, and—in some cases—big neck frills. These looked like defense features, but some were so impressive that they were probably partly for show, like deer antlers.

Kentrosaurus
Stegosaurs such as this *Kentrosaurus* had rows of plates and spikes on their backs. They helped these animals recognize each other from a distance.

Each stegosaur had a different pattern of plates.

An inflatable crest is lighter than bone.

Muttaburrasaurus
This plant-eater's snout was enlarged into a hollow bulge that might have supported a showy crest. The crest could have been inflatable, forming a resonating chamber to make the animal's calls boom out louder.

The sharp horn kept predators at bay.

Centrosaurus

This rhinolike dinosaur was about 20 ft (6 m) long, and had a big, bony frill covering its neck. The frill was too ornate to be purely defensive, but its nose horn might have been used for defense.

Irritator

The large, sail-like fin on *Irritator's* back was supported by extensions of its backbone. It made this fish-eater look a lot bigger, impressing its enemies and rivals. *Irritator* may also have had a small crest on the top of its head.

The sail may have been vividly colored.

The hollow crest may have worked like a trumpet.

Parasaurolophus

Some duck-billed dinosaurs had long crests on their heads. *Parasaurolophus* had the longest, supported by a bony tube linked to its windpipe that made this dinosaur's calls sound louder.

Spiky ceratopsians

Some of the most spectacular dinosaurs belonged to a group of heavily built, beaked plant-eaters called the ceratopsians. Many had long spikes and horns on their heads, and elaborate bony frills extending over their necks. These were partly for show but also had some defensive value.

Protoceratops

About the size of a pig, *Protoceratops* lived in the late Cretaceous Period. Scientists have found the remains of at least two types, with different-shaped neck frills, and some think that these were males and females.

Einiosaurus

Much bigger and heavier than *Protoceratops*, this ceratopsian had a hooked, rhinolike horn on its nose and two long horns on its neck frill. Like other ceratopsians, it had a parrotlike beak that was supported by special bones at the tips of both its lower and upper jaws.

Styracosaurus

The name of this dinosaur means "spiked lizard," referring to the spectacular crown of spikes around its neck frill. Its sharp, scissorlike teeth were perfect for slicing up its tough plant food.

Pentaceratops

The size of an elephant, *Pentaceratops* had a huge, very imposing neck frill that was probably brightly patterned. It lived in the late Cretaceous in what is now the United States, where its fossils have been found in New Mexico.

Triceratops

The most well-known of the ceratopsians lived at the very end of the dinosaur era in North America, where it was very common. Despite its dangerous-looking horns, it was killed and eaten by the massively powerful *Tyrannosaurus rex*.

FINE FEATHERS

Recently discovered fossils show that many theropod dinosaurs had feathers, and that some of them were very long. A few fossils even preserve traces of bright colors and eye-catching patterns.

These arm feathers may have had a practical use.

Toothless hunter

All four limbs had long, decorative feathers.

Ground-living predator

Fuzzy dinosaur

Each primitive feather was like a single, slender hair.

Citipati
Fossil remains of the feathered dinosaur *Citipati* show that it used its feathery arms to keep its eggs warm, like a chicken. The long feathers may also have been brightly colored.

Sinornithosaurus
A group of theropods called the maniraptorans had long arms covered with birdlike feathers. However, for most of these dinosaurs, the feathers were only for show.

Sinosauropteryx
Well-preserved fossils of this small hunter show evidence of primitive hairlike feathers. They would have formed a fuzzy, protective coat, like the fur of a cat.

The first dinosaur feathers were like hair, but many dinosaurs grew feathers just like those of modern birds.

The fan of feathers sprouted from a long, bony tail.

Fast-running, feathered omnivore

The front limbs had strong, curved claws.

Tree-dweller

All four limbs may have acted as wings.

The wing feathers were just like those of modern birds.

Caudipteryx
This turkey-sized maniraptoran had an impressive fan of tail feathers. It also had long feathers on its arms. Since it could not fly, these may have been for display to rivals and partners.

Microraptor
Small tree-climbers such as Microraptor may have been able to use their long-feathered limbs to glide from tree to tree. This allowed them to avoid the dangers of the forest floor.

Early flying bird

Archaeopteryx
Some maniraptorans developed the ability to flap their wings and became birds. Archaeopteryx, a weak flier, was one of the first. Later birds evolved into more capable fliers.

Corythosaurus

Like other duck-billed ornithopods of the late Cretaceous, *Corythosaurus* chewed its leafy food with very efficient grinding teeth. Chewing made the food much easier to digest.

SUCCESS STORY

The ornithopods were some of the most successful dinosaurs. The earliest were small, beaked plant-eaters that stood on their back legs. Many later ones were bigger, with highly specialized chewing teeth.

Long hind legs and feet show that it was built for speed.

Hypsilophodon

Slender and agile, *Hypsilophodon* was typical of the smaller, primitive ornithopods. It fed on low-growing plants, and could swiftly flee from danger on its hind legs.

Tail was
extremely long.

Jaws had
leaf-shaped teeth.

Tenontosaurus

Much bigger than *Hypsilophodon*, this
animal supported its bulky body on all
four feet part of the time. It had few
defenses and may have lived in herds for
protection from hungry hunters.

Iguanodon

The size of an elephant,
Iguanodon spent most
of its time walking on
all fours. However,
its hands had long,
mobile fingers and
thumbs armed with
sharp spikes.

· Thumb spike was
about 6 in (14 cm) long. ·

67

Eggs and young

As far as we know, **all dinosaurs laid eggs. Many buried them** under heaps of leaves, while others **laid them in nests on the ground**. A few dinosaurs may have let their newly hatched **young fend for themselves**, but some took care of them.

What were the eggs like?

Either round or oval, dinosaur eggs had hard, brittle shells like birds' eggs. The biggest were the size of footballs, but that's tiny when compared to the animals that laid them. This shows that dinosaurs grew very fast.

What was inside them?

Some fossilized eggs contain the remains of baby dinosaurs. This reconstruction of an intact *Troodon* egg shows how the baby was curled up inside the eggshell, with its head tucked between its long back legs.

How many eggs were laid?

All the dinosaur nests discovered so far contained a lot of eggs—up to 20 in some cases. This allowed dinosaurs to breed much faster than modern big animals such as elephants and rhinoceroses.

How were the eggs kept warm?

Burying eggs under heaps of leaves kept them warm, because the leaves created heat as they decayed. But the fossil remains of small dinosaurs such as *Citipati* sitting on nests show that some incubated their eggs using body heat, just like most modern birds.

Who stole the eggs?

The eggs and helpless babies would have been easy prey for small hunters such as these *Deinonychus*, if they could get past the parents. The fossil remains of such egg thieves are often found near dinosaur nesting sites.

Bringing up baby

You look much **cuter** than me!

Giant nesting site

A dinosaur nesting ground in South America contained thousands of *Saltasaurus* eggs. Hundreds of females laid the eggs, buried them in warm ground, and probably waited for them to hatch.

Most **dinosaurs** died before

Some dinosaurs, including most big hunters, lived in separate family groups. But others gathered in **breeding colonies**, all laying their eggs at the same time and raising their young together. Many were probably very **good parents**.

Caring parents

Huge *Maiasaura* breeding colonies found in Montana prove that these big plant-eaters nested close together for safety. Fossils of the babies show that they lived on food brought to them by their parents.

Growing up together

As soon as they were old enough to walk, young dinosaurs would start looking for their own food. But they stuck together for defense, because some big hunters could eat a baby *Saltasaurus* for breakfast!

they were **30 years** old.

ON THE MOVE

Some dinosaurs lived **alone** or in **pairs**, but many lived and traveled in **groups** or **huge herds**. Most were PLANT-EATERS that could *share plentiful food.* But it's also likely that some MEAT-EATERS *hunted in packs* to catch big prey.

TRACKWAYS

We assume that some dinosaurs traveled in herds because their **footprints** have survived as fossilized trackways. Some show **dozens of animals** of different sizes walking together in the same direction.

EDMONTOSAURUS

Herds **run out of food** if they don't stay on the move, and traveling together has always been **safer** than traveling alone. Dinosaurs such as *Edmontosaurus* probably had the same way of life.

Big herds of **Edmontosaurus** once roamed the plains of **North America**.

Almost 66 million years ago, a catastrophe ended the Mesozoic Era, wiping out the giant dinosaurs and many other animals, including the spectacular pterosaurs. But some animals such as birds and mammals survived, and their descendants live all around us.

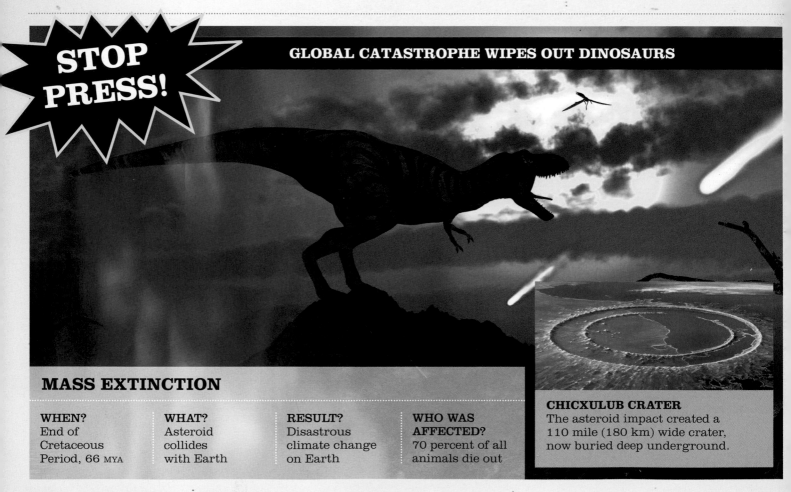

STOP PRESS!

GLOBAL CATASTROPHE WIPES OUT DINOSAURS

MASS EXTINCTION

WHEN?	**WHAT?**	**RESULT?**	**WHO WAS AFFECTED?**
End of Cretaceous Period, 66 MYA	Asteroid collides with Earth	Disastrous climate change on Earth	70 percent of all animals die out

CHICXULUB CRATER
The asteroid impact created a 110 mile (180 km) wide crater, now buried deep underground.

Death from the skies

We know that Earth was struck by a huge asteroid or comet at roughly the same time as the giant dinosaurs vanished. The impact caused an explosion that was two million times as powerful as the biggest nuclear bomb ever detonated. It would have devastated a vast area and caused climate chaos all over the world.

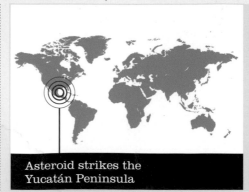

Asteroid strikes the Yucatán Peninsula

IMPACT ZONE
The object that hit Earth was at least 6 miles (10 km) wide. It struck the north coast of the Mexican Yucatán Peninsula, near a point that is now the small town of Chicxulub.

AN ERA

Was it a volcanic eruption?

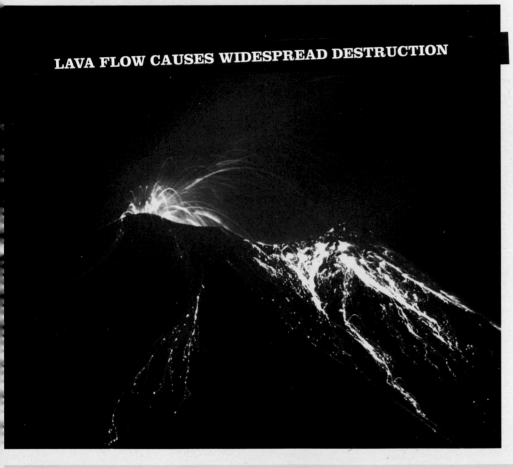

LAVA FLOW CAUSES WIDESPREAD DESTRUCTION

Many scientists think that the asteroid impact killed off the big dinosaurs. But the world was already reeling from another disaster—colossal volcanic eruptions in India that lasted for thousands of years. They produced vast quantities of lava, and would have filled the atmosphere with dust and poisonous gases.

Volcanic eruptions in western India

DISASTER AREA
The lava from the volcanoes cooled to create a layer of basalt rock 1.2 miles (2 km) thick. This covers a huge area of India known as the Deccan Traps.

SURVIVOR ALERT

Some live on

Big marine reptiles such as the plesiosaurs were wiped out, but sea turtles survived. So did tortoises, lizards, snakes, and crocodiles.

For reasons we don't understand, birds resembling this Cretaceous *Ichthyornis* survived while all the other dinosaurs perished.

Small mammals related to the mouse-sized *Nemegtbaatar* escaped. Their descendants evolved into the mammals we know today.

Protostega

Ichthyornis

Nemegtbaatar

LIFE AFTER THE EXTINCTION

The catastrophe that killed the giant dinosaurs left the world in chaos. But over the years, its deadly effects began to wear off. **Life started flourishing again**, and the surviving animals and plants evolved into many new forms, replacing those that had vanished. **It was the new world of the Cenozoic Era.**

Tropical rain forest

CLIMATE CHANGE

After the extinction, the global climate got colder, but temperatures rose dramatically about 55 million years ago. After this warm period, the world started cooling again, and about 2.5 million years ago ice started forming at the poles. This was the beginning of a series of ice ages, with the last really cold phase ending just 12,000 years ago.

Arctic ice

PLANT LIFE

During the warm phase of the early Cenozoic Era, tropical rain forests of trees such as dawn redwoods covered vast areas of the world, as far north as Canada. Over time, the cooling climate gradually created drier conditions with colder winters and many of the forests gave way to dry grasslands.

Dawn redwood leaves

Gastornis

AGE OF MAMMALS

Mammals had been around for as long as the dinosaurs, but they became a major part of the wildlife only after the giant dinosaurs were wiped out. They evolved into many types, including bats, giant sloths, mammoths, and the fearsome saber-toothed cat *Smilodon*.

Icaronycteris

Smilodon

FEATHERED SURVIVORS

A few birds survived the extinction. They went on to evolve into many forms, including the giant, flightless *Gastornis* and vulture like *Argentavis*. Most modern types of birds had appeared by 25 million years ago.

Argentavis

An Australopithecus afarensis family

OUR ANCESTORS

The first humanlike creatures, known to scientists as *Australopithecus*, walked upright on the African tropical grasslands about five million years ago. *Homo sapiens*—modern humans just like us—appeared in Africa about 200,000 years ago. Before long, they were crafting the tools that were to help create modern civilization.

Stone-age ax head

GLOSSARY

ancestor a species from which other species have evolved.

ankylosaurs armored, four-legged, plant-eating dinosaurs with bony plates.

archosaurs a group of animals that includes dinosaurs, birds, pterosaurs, and crocodiles.

asteroid a large space rock smaller than a dwarf planet.

browse to feed on plants other than grasses.

camouflage colors and patterns that make an animal hard to see.

carnivore a species that eats other animals.

Cenozoic the era that followed the age of dinosaurs, from 66 MYA to the present.

ceratopsians the horned dinosaurs, usually with horns on their faces and bony frills covering their necks.

colony a large group of animals living together, often for breeding.

comet a big lump of rock, ice, and dust traveling through space.

coprolites fossilized feces.

Cretaceous the third of three periods making up the Mesozoic Era, from 145 to 66 million years ago.

evolution the process by which living things change over time.

extinct having completely died out.

herbivore a species that mainly eats plants.

ice age a time when Earth has large areas of ice near the poles.

ichthyosaurs a group of dolphinlike marine reptiles.

incubate to keep eggs warm so they develop and hatch.

Jurassic the second of three periods making up the Mesozoic Era, from 200 to 145 million years ago.

lava rock that has erupted from a volcano in liquid, molten form.

mammal a furry animal that feeds its newborn young on milk.

marginocephalians a dinosaur group that includes the horned dinosaurs and boneheads.

marine relating to the ocean or sea.

mass extinction a disaster that causes the disappearance of many types of life.

Mesozoic the era known as the age of dinosaurs, from 251 to 66 million years ago.

microbe a living thing too small to be seen without a microscope.

mimic to copy, or a thing that copies something else.

MYA million years ago.

omnivore an animal that eats a wide variety of plant and animal foods.

ornithischian one of the two main divisions of dinosaurs.

ornithopods a group of plant-eating dinosaurs that mostly walked on their hind legs and were not armored.

pachycephalosaurs thick-skulled, "boneheaded" dinosaurs.

petrified turned to stone.

plesiosaurs a group of marine reptiles with four long flippers; many had long necks (see image below).

predator an animal that kills other animals for food.

prey an animal that is eaten by another animal.

primitive describes an early or less highly evolved form.

prosauropods the first long-necked, plant-eating dinosaurs, which lived before the sauropods.

pterosaurs flying reptiles with wings of stretched skin that lived during the Mesozoic Era.

rain forest an evergreen forest that grows in warm, wet regions.

replica an exact copy.

reptiles the group of animals that includes turtles, lizards, crocodiles, snakes, pterosaurs, and dinosaurs.

saurischian one of the two main divisions of dinosaurs.

sauropodomorphs the group that includes prosauropods and true sauropods.

sauropods long-necked, plant-eating dinosaurs that evolved from the prosauropods.

shellfish clams, oysters, crabs, and similar hard-shelled sea creatures.

species a particular type of living thing that can breed with others of the same type.

squid a sea animal related to octopuses.

stegosaurs the group of armored dinosaurs with large plates and spines on their backs.

supercontinent a huge landmass made up of many continents that have joined together.

theropods saurischian dinosaurs that were nearly all meat-eaters.

thyreophorans armored stegosaurs and ankylosaurs.

titanosaurs a group of sauropods that evolved in the Cretaceous Period.

trackway a trail of fossil footprints.

tree rings annual rings of growth in trees that also show the tree's age.

Triassic the first of three periods making up the Mesozoic Era, from 251 to 200 million years ago.

troodontids dinosaurs including and closely related to *Troodon*.

tropical refers to a warm climate, or to the warm part of the world near the equator.

tyrannosaurs dinosaurs including and closely related to *Tyrannosaurus*.

vertebrate an animal with an internal skeleton and backbone.

windpipe the breathing tube that connects the throat to the lungs.

INDEX

CREDITS

The publisher would like to thank the following people for their assistance in the preparation of this book: Vaibhav Rastogi for design assistance and Carron Brown for proofreading and compiling the index.

Smithsonian Enterprises:
Carol LeBlanc, Senior Vice President
Brigid Ferraro, Director of Licensing
Ellen Nanney, Licensing Manager
Kealy Wilson, Product Development Manager

Smithsonian Project Coordinator:
Kealy Wilson